DIABETES

DIABETES

by Sarah R. Riedman

FRANKLIN WATTS
NEW YORK | LONDON | TORONTO | SYDNEY | 1980
A FIRST BOOK

Illustrations courtesy of Vantage Art, Inc.

Photographs courtesy of: Wide World Photos: pp. 7, 51 (left); World Health Organization by J. Gordon: p. 20; Michal Heron/Monkmeyer Press Photo Service: p. 23; W. B. Carter: p. 51 (right).

Library of Congress Cataloging in Publication Data

Riedman, Sarah Regal, 1902–
Diabetes.

(A First book)
Bibliography: p.
Includes index.
SUMMARY: Explains the nature of diabetes, its causes, complications, and how to live comfortably with the disease.
1. Diabetes—Juvenile literature. 2. Diabetes in children—Juvenile literature. [1. Diabetes. 2. Diseases] I. Title.
RC660.R485   616.4'62   80–14473
ISBN 0–531–04162–X

ACKNOWLEDGMENTS

The author is deeply indebted to Renee M. Marsteller, B.S.N.R. for reviewing the manuscript and for her unstinting help in more ways than can be listed. Mrs. Marsteller is a founder, and member of the Board of Directors of the Indian River Chapter of the Juvenile Diabetes Foundation, and its Corresponding Secretary. From her professional and family experience she is no stranger to the disease, and has given freely of her knowledge in conducting educational programs in hospitals. She is experienced in counseling diabetics and those who are charged with their care. Her tireless efforts in promoting basic research into the causes, means of preventing the disastrous complications and efforts that may lead to a cure of the disease have borne fruit in recent advances that have been reported.

My heartfelt thanks also to the children with diabetes and their parents, as well as the adults with the disease who graciously consented to interviews. My appreciation of their courage in accepting and coping with a life-long disorder has thereby been enormously enhanced.

S.R.R.

Contents

Chapter 1
1 WHAT'S WRONG WITH JAMIE, DOCTOR?

Chapter 2
4 WHAT DIABETES IS AND ISN'T

Chapter 3
10 INSULIN: BLOOD SUGAR REGULATOR

Chapter 4
14 WHAT HAPPENS IN DIABETES

Chapter 5
18 LIFETIME CARE

Chapter 6
27 DIABETIC EMERGENCIES: TWO OPPOSITES

Chapter 7
32 WHEN ADULTS GET DIABETES

Chapter 8
39 COMPLICATIONS OF A COMPLICATED DISEASE

Chapter 9
43 LIVING A LIFETIME WITH DIABETES

Chapter 10
48 RESEARCH DIRECTIONS TODAY

55 Glossary

58 Further Reading

60 Index

DIABETES

Chapter 1
WHAT'S WRONG
WITH JAMIE, DOCTOR?

Jamie's certificate from his doctor said he was in good health when he entered kindergarten shortly after his fifth birthday. A few weeks later he came down with a fever and a respiratory illness, described as "summer flu," due to what the doctor called a Coxsackie virus. When he was thought well enough to go back to school, some worrisome changes came over him. His mother told the doctor that Jamie was urinating much too often during the day, and what was unusual, Jamie couldn't "hold his water" at night. He kept drinking a lot yet could not quench a constant thirst. He complained of being hungry, craving sweets, and feeling weak. And according to the doctor's records, Jamie had lost weight since his last visit.

What was wrong? The doctor suspected diabetes but would have to do a test or two to be sure. First he checked a urine specimen for sugar. The test was positive: sugar in the urine, which is not normal. Along with Jamie's other symptoms, the presence of sugar in the urine added up to more than just a suspicion of diabetes. A blood test showed that the amount of sugar carried in Jamie's blood was also much higher than normal. The doctor then was certain of the diagnosis as *diabetes mellitus,* still commonly called the "sugar diabetes."

The doctor promptly prescribed treatment, because diabetes, especially in children, calls for immediate, and constant strict attention. Jamie will need insulin every day for the rest of his life, the doctor said. He would work out a schedule of when and how much insulin Jamie would require, as well as what foods he should eat and which he should avoid. He stressed that Jamie should eat at the first pangs of hunger and before exercise. Why this special regimen for Jamie? Specific treatment is designed for each individual because no diabetic is exactly the same as anyone else with this disease.

While impressing Jamie's mother with the seriousness of diabetes, for which there is no cure, the doctor at the same time reassured her that today it can be controlled with insulin and the right foods, in the right amount, at the right time. With proper care he would be able to play, attend school, and grow, much like his schoolmates.

Sixty years ago no such reassurance could have been given to a child with Jamie's condition. Children with this wasting disease died within a year or two after its onset— but not because it was a new disease then, nor its symptoms unrecognized. Actually, diabetes is one of the oldest known, having been described over 3,000 years ago in an Egyptian papyrus scroll. Aretaeus, a Greek physician wrote in the first century A.D.: "Diabetes is a strange disease. . . . Life is painful; thirst unquenchable; drinking excessive. . . . Death is speedy."

[2

Today things don't have to get to that stage. The symptoms are readily recognized as in Jamie's case. His doctor is certain to explain to his parents the nature of the disease. They will need to fully understand the details of careful daily care to keep the symptoms under control. Jamie himself will learn to *feel* signs of poor control and how to correct the problem. As he grows older he will also learn to gradually take over the responsibility of his own routine care. But throughout his childhood his doctor, as part of the team with Jamie and his parents, will keep a check on his health. From time to time the doctor will be available to answer Jamie's questions about what he may or may not eat at a birthday party or outing, what sports he may play, or whether he may go on field trips. The doctor will advise Jamie on how to avoid an imbalance of blood sugar and its consequences during an infection or a tooth extraction. For diabetes is a complicated disease with occasional ups and downs, and it is not a disease that is outgrown. One must be prepared to live with it for life.

Chapter 2
WHAT DIABETES IS AND ISN'T

What is diabetes? It is easier to say what it isn't, so let's begin with what it is *not*. It is not one of the common childhood infections such as measles, whooping cough, chicken pox, or scarlet fever. It is not "catching." It cannot be prevented by vaccination, and it does not run its course within days, weeks, or even months. Nor is it caused by eating the wrong kind of food, or the lack of a vitamin or other essential nutrient. Its cause is not known, which may be only one reason why there is no cure for it.

Diabetes takes its name from two Greek words combined to mean "siphon" or "run through," describing the enormous loss of water in the large quantities of urine. Noting the sweetness of the urine, the Romans added a second word, making the full name *diabetes mellitus; mellitus* is the Latin name for honey.

The particular sugar appearing in the urine of diabetics is called *glucose.* Glucose comes from food, not only from *carbohydrates* (sugar and starches). A certain percent also comes from the digestion of *proteins* and *fats.* Glucose is the body's chief fuel which it burns or *oxidizes* to provide energy. A reserve supply of it is stored in the liver and muscles; as needed it is released into the blood and carried to the tissues. None of it is excreted. Any excess is stored as *glycogen,* a complex carbohydrate, or converted into fat and stored as body fat.

Diabetes is a chronic condition in which the body cannot utilize glucose as an energy source. It is classed as a *metabolic* disorder, which is to say that the body chemistry is abnormal, resulting in the inability to utilize food properly. Insulin is the hormone which enables the body to use glucose, and indirectly, all food. Insulin is produced in the pancreas, a gland which lies behind the stomach.

When diabetes occurs suddenly, as is usual in children, the pancreas for some reason either stops making insulin or does not produce nearly enough to handle all the glucose. The effect of insulin lack is as if the spark that sets off the burning of glucose is suddenly missing.

What triggers the sudden lack of insulin at a particular time, as in Jamie's case? Perhaps it is set off by a viral infection. We do not really know. But it is believed that such an infection, the stress of a surgical operation, great shock from a severe injury, or a shattering emotional upset could bring on the symptoms. However touched off, diabetes may or may not occur in persons who have a history of diabetes in the family, and have inherited a tendency to the disease. This does not mean that a diabetic parent necessarily hands it down to the child like the blood type, according to the laws of heredity. Diabetes is not a hereditary disorder. A family history usually, but not always, reveals that a grandparent or other blood relative has or had the disease.

[5

HOW COMMON IS DIABETES?

Diabetes occurs nearly all over the world. In the United States, it is estimated that 10 to 12 million people have diabetes. Approximately one to two million (including at least 500,000 children) have to take insulin. The disease is said to be on the increase. There are probably 2 million adults who are not even aware that they have diabetes until a blood test reveals it during an examination for some other complaint. The condition is rare in Eskimos, infrequent in blacks in Africa, and not commonly found in Oriental people, especially the Japanese. It is uncommon in Asian Indians, but Asians who have migrated to South Africa and changed their lifestyle (those who eat more and do less physical work) are more prone to become diabetic. This would indicate that besides the genetic factor (heredity), other so-called environmental factors are involved.

WHO GETS DIABETES?

Anyone may get diabetes. It occurs in both sexes and at any age from infancy to past middle life. It happens more often in persons with relatives who have diabetes, in the middle-aged and elderly, and in people who are excessively overweight.

A child whose mother or father is diabetic runs some risk of getting the disease. There is less chance if the parent does not have the disease but is a *carrier,* meaning that he or she has the gene but not the expression of it as the full-blown disorder. The greatest risk would be for the offspring of two diabetics. If both parents have it, the chance of the child having it is thought to be about one in eight, or 12 percent. But the chances of getting it are much less when the

Pushing off for the backstroke at a camp for diabetic children. While diabetes is a serious and complicated disease, with the proper care and attention most diabetics are able to lead a full and active life.

relative is a grandparent, an aunt, an uncle, or a first cousin. Children of diabetics who do not develop diabetes may pass the trait on to their own children. There are many more adults who develop diabetes after the age of 45, and more frequently if they are also obese.

THERE ARE
TWO TYPES
OF DIABETES

Diabetes is by no means equally severe in all diabetics; it depends upon the degree of insulin deficiency. For example, the pancreas may produce sufficient insulin for the carbohydrate intake, except during periods of overindulgence in sweets and starchy foods, in a person who maintains a close-to-standard weight for height and age, and is on a well-balanced diet.

There are, however, two main types of diabetes: 1) *Juvenile-onset:* this type, as in Jamie's case, starts suddenly any time before the age of thirty-five. 2) *Maturity-onset:* in this type, age is indeed a major factor, and the disease occurs about nine times more frequently after the ages of 40 to 45.

In juvenile diabetes, there is a total lack of insulin. People with juvenile diabetes must have insulin by injection to live, and are therefore *insulin-dependent.* In most older adults insulin production may be deficient or less effective in the obese, but their diabetes can often be controlled without insulin injections. This type of diabetes is called *non-insulin-dependent.* Many adults, however, may also require insulin.

The differences between the two main types of diabetes are not merely age of onset. Other differences in causes and treatment, are shown in the table at right.

[8

STRIKING DIFFERENCES
BETWEEN
THE TYPES OF DIABETES

Juvenile-onset	*Maturity-onset*
Onset is sudden; symptoms easily evident	Onset creeps up; sometimes called the "sneaky disease"
Overweight is not a factor	Obesity is a contributing factor; as many as 85 percent are overweight
Need for insulin is absolute	Few need insulin
Dietary treatment *alone* does not control	Diet and exercise may control more than one third of the cases
Oral blood sugar-lowering drugs (not for children)	Diet and drugs control in rest of cases
Loss of control emergencies occur more often	Loss of control emergencies are not common
Degenerative changes in blood vessels (leading to impaired vision and hearing) may begin a dozen or more years after onset	Blood vessel changes may already be present when diabetes is discovered

Chapter 3
INSULIN: BLOOD
SUGAR REGULATOR

Like all hormones, insulin is produced in living cells and released directly into the bloodstream. It circulates through the blood to various parts of the body where its special job is to govern the utilization of glucose.

Some hormones are essential to life; others, such as the one that controls growth or the one that stimulates the flow of milk from the mammary glands are not. Insulin is one of those essential to life. This is why children with diabetes are insulin-dependent. Insulin is a protein, and like other proteins, its building blocks are aminoacids arranged in two chains. Since it is a protein, it would be useless to take it by mouth, because it would be digested in the stomach and intestine. It therefore must be injected so that it gets to the blood intact.

A GLAND WITH TWO JOBS

Insulin is made in the pancreas, but the pancreas has two different jobs. In fact, it belongs to two different systems: the digestive and endocrine (hormone forming) systems. We have here a gland *within* a gland, not readily separated. The digestive function of the pancreas is to produce pancreatic juice, containing digestive enzymes. The product leaves by duct or tube into the intestine where food is digested. The production of insulin is the work of totally different kinds of cells, distinct from the enzyme-producing cells of the pancreas.

Over a century ago it was discovered that scattered through the pancreas are microscopic islands of special cells. Named for their discoverer, they are known as the *Islets of Langerhans.* About a million of them are surrounded by sacs of pancreatic cells. The islets form about 5 percent of the weight of the pancreas.

Some twenty years after the discovery of the islets, two German scientists removed the pancreas from several dogs. A laboratory worker charged with the care of these animals noticed that flies were swarming around the urine of the dogs which had become ill following the removal of the pancreas. The scientists concluded that the flies were after the sugar escaping in their urine. More than that, although the dogs were eating a great deal, they were losing weight rapidly. They were also thirsty as well as hungry. The unburned sugar was escaping together with a large quantity of water in which it was dissolved. Before long the dogs died, as you can now guess, from diabetes.

Later studies convinced scientists that it was the islets that manufactured a special product, which if it could be extracted, could be used to treat diabetes. (Much later the product was named *insulin,* from *insula,* the Latin for "island" or "islet.")

Doctors tried feeding pancreas to their diabetic patients; experimenters tried to extract the insulin from the

[11

whole pancreas. These attempts failed because the insulin was digested by the enzymes produced by the pancreatic cells. How to separate the two was the crucial question.

1921: THE YEAR
OF THE BREAKTHROUGH

Dr. Frederick Banting, a Canadian physician in Toronto, formulated a plan to separate these two sets of cells. His idea was to make the enzyme-producing cells of the pancreas die. He was soon joined in his experiments by Charles Best, a medical student about to be graduated from the University of Toronto.

Success was not immediate. But after several trials of tying off the pancreatic duct and waiting just the right amount of time (four but not six weeks), the pancreatic cells shriveled and died, but the island cells remained intact. They ground up the tissue, made the extract, and with the help of Dr. James Collip, a biochemist, prepared the precious substance in pure form. They injected it into a dog dying from diabetes after the removal of its pancreas. The dog began to recover, and samples of its blood showed that the sugar was dropping to its normal level. With continued injections of the extract the experimenters were able to keep the diabetic dog alive.

It is for this discovery, which saved many from the brink of death, that the Nobel Prize in Medicine and Physiology was awarded in 1923. Today insulin is the lifesaver for millions of diabetics. Let's see how insulin works.

EATING SIGNALS THE
RELEASE OF INSULIN

As soon as you eat, the islet cells begin to convert stored inactive granules into active insulin. It is discharged into the

[12

bloodstream. It arrives there just as glucose after digestion from the meal is ready to be absorbed from the intestine into the blood. Together, glucose and insulin reach the liver where the excess glucose is dropped off. The liver is the storage pantry; its cells convert glucose into *glycogen* or "animal starch." Insulin is necessary for this conversion. The remaining glucose, along with the insulin, streams through to the cells of all the tissues. Here insulin acts as the "spark" which "ignites" or starts off the oxidation of glucose, releasing energy. It also moves amino acids (from digested protein) into the cells to build tissue protein.

Insulin is produced by one of the two kinds of cells in the islets—the *beta cells.* Simple sugar is released into the blood as needed with the help of another islet hormone prepared by the *alpha cells.* This hormone is *glucagon,* which works in the opposite way from insulin. Together the two hormones regulate the process by which the blood sugar level remains remarkably stable—at around 100 milligrams per 100 milliliters of blood. It is usually written as 100 mg percent. A level below 80 mg and above 120 mg is either borderline or abnormal in some people.

Thus, insulin serves as the body's signal during feasting to lower the blood sugar. Glucagon serves as the body's signal during fasting to raise blood sugar by discharging it from the liver. When eating normally, the sugar level of the non-diabetic always remains steady, without a thought on the person's part. Not so in the insulin-dependent person.

Chapter 4
WHAT HAPPENS
IN DIABETES

GLUCOSE PILE-UP
IN THE BLOOD

After a meal is digested, glucose is absorbed into the blood. When insulin is totally lacking or even insufficient, the blood sugar keeps rising above the normal level, because the body cannot use it. The pile-up of sugar in the blood is called *hyperglycemia. Hyper* means "high," *glyc* refers to "glucose," and *emia* stands for "blood." The unused glucose is carried to the kidneys. The job of the kidneys is to rid the body of wastes, but in the presence of excess blood glucose, the kidneys treat it as waste.

GLUCOSE SPILL-OVER
IN THE URINE

The kidneys may be compared to a dam which holds back the normal amount of sugar in the blood. But when it rises above the top of the dam, it spills over into the urine. This condi-

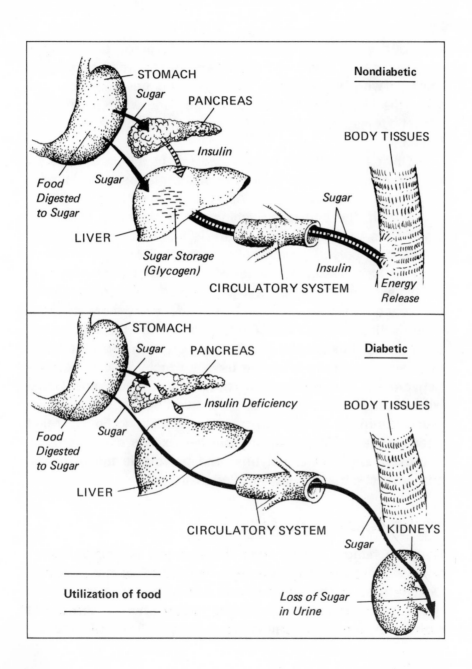

STOMACH

Sugar

PANCREAS

Insulin

Nondiabetic

BODY TISSUES

Food Digested to Sugar

Sugar

LIVER

Sugar Storage (Glycogen)

Sugar

Insulin

CIRCULATORY SYSTEM

Energy Release

STOMACH

Sugar

PANCREAS

Insulin Deficiency

Diabetic

BODY TISSUES

Food Digested to Sugar

Sugar

LIVER

CIRCULATORY SYSTEM

Sugar

KIDNEYS

Utilization of food

Loss of Sugar in Urine

tion is described as *glycosuria.* The level of blood sugar that will cause this overflow differs in different people. In children with diabetes, the urine may be positive for sugar when the blood sugar tops 120 mg percent, while in an older diabetic it may reach over 220 mg percent before it spills over the dam.

Obviously, glucose is excreted not in lumps or crystals but dissolved in water. To wash out the glucose, the kidneys draw water from the blood. As long as the blood sugar remains high, the constant flushing out takes more and more water from the blood. Thus, there is frequent and excessive urination, or *polyuria,* the name for this symptom.

The loss of large quantities of water is not just wasteful; it upsets still another balance in the blood. The blood becomes too concentrated or "thick." It is made even more concentrated with wastes called *ketone bodies* from the incomplete oxidation of fats. In the process of restoring the blood volume, water is drawn from the tissues which, in turn, become dehydrated. This is felt as dryness in the mouth and throat where thirst is experienced. This thirst is known as *polydipsia.* Drinking to quench this thirst does not bring relief because the cycle of washing out the excess sugar remains unbroken. Glycosuria, polyuria, and polydipsia make up the characteristic triad of uncontrolled diabetes.

TISSUE HUNGER AND FATIGUE

Normally hunger is felt when the stomach is empty. Sometimes it makes itself known by a "growling" of the stomach. Despite food in the stomach and lots of sugar in the blood, the diabetic experiences a kind of nagging hunger that is not satisfied by food. It is called tissue hunger. The cells are unable to burn sugar, and do not release energy; the person then feels tired, weak, and even dizzy and faint. The dizziness and faintness are the result of failure of the brain to utilize its only fuel—glucose. Unlike muscles that can burn fat and later also protein, the brain must have glucose as fuel.

Without adequate treatment, the diabetic loses weight as well as energy. Throughout life, even during periods of growth, the cells steadily wear down and are simultaneously repaired or restored. When energy release fails, growth stops and the wasting of the tissues means weight loss.

You will recognize that all these changes were the very signs that brought Jamie to the doctor. He is lucky that these symptoms could be reversed by a plan of treatment the doctor prescribed. A crucial part of that treatment is insulin injected regularly and in amounts to balance food intake.

DANGERS OF
INADEQUATE CONTROL

Juvenile diabetes, by its startlingly sudden onset and rapid march of distressing symptoms, calls for prompt and rigorous treatment. The regimen must be maintained continuously, not only to reverse the symptoms, but to prevent complications from tissue damage over a number of years.

The slower onset of diabetes of the older adult type, so often unrecognized for years in some people, carries the same risk of serious complications. In fact, it may be the complications that bring the person to the doctor in the first place.

For both the young and the elderly, *diabetes mellitus* is a serious, chronic disease. However, with the right treatment not only can it be controlled, but complications may be prevented, reduced, or at least put off.

Chapter 5
LIFETIME CARE

When a child is ill with a fever or an infection, we try to help him or her get well as soon as possible. With diabetes the task is to help the child *stay well* all the time, every day throughout life.

Good health in the diabetic means being free from symptoms by preventing their recurrence, and avoiding complications resulting from poor care. To achieve these ends, the prescribed plan of care can be said to rest on a firm four-legged stool. It involves: 1) good diet; 2) carefully regulated insulin injections; 3) suitable kinds and amounts of exercise; 4) the daily testing of urine. If any of the four legs breaks, the stool collapses and diabetes is out of control.

Let's see how the regimen works in the life of a particular diabetic child.

[18

A DAY IN ANDREA'S LIFE

Andrea is eleven. She became diabetic four years ago. Her parents do not have diabetes, which is not unusual. Of course, it is possible that either one will develop the disease sometime during middle age.

By now Andrea has learned how to do certain things for herself to stay in control; things that her parents had to do for her at first.

URINE TESTING

Every morning, Andrea starts her day by testing her urine for sugar, and if highly positive, by testing also for ketone. This tells her whether she will need to increase her amount of insulin. Her daily record for the month shows that no adjustment in the insulin had been required, even though on some days there were traces of sugar in her urine.

There are two commonly used tests for sugar in the urine: the tablet method and the stick method. Andrea uses the tablet method. With a medicine dropper, she puts 10 drops of water and 5 drops of urine into a tiny beaker, and drops 1 tablet into the mixture. She waits 15 seconds until the "boiling" stops; then she checks the tint in the beaker against the graded shades on a chart. *Blue* means 0 percent sugar (test is negative); *green* means ¼ percent (a trace); *cloudy green* is ½ percent (1+ sugar); *orange* is 2 percent (4+ sugar).

Unless the test shows 4+ sugar she does not have to test for ketone. The test for ketone is similar, but it involves the use of a different tablet. These tests, as well as keeping a daily record of the results on a card taped to the bathroom wall, are the procedures to test for sugar and ketone in the urine. Andrea's test is negative today. Her doctor wants her also to test the

urine before the evening meal. For someone else the regimen may call for testing at bedtime, or even four times a day.

EXACTNESS: THE RULE
IN THE INSULIN STORY

Next, Andrea is ready for her insulin injection. At first, her mother or one other person trained to do it gave her the injection. After her eighth birthday Andrea began to learn to inject herself, having learned the steps: sterilize the skin with alcohol-moistened cotton; bunch the skin between the thumb and forefinger; holding the needle at a right angle, inject into the bunched up skin. Andrea knows the areas of the body most suitable for injections: the thighs, upper arms, buttocks or abdomen. She knows *not* to inject below the knee or in a spot in the upper arm where tendons or a nerve must be avoided. It is also important to rotate the injection sites about once a month. Giving insulin for too long on the same site may cause problems, such as indentations ("pitting") or thickened, unsightly spots. Worse yet, the insulin would not be absorbed properly through the thickened skin.

Testing their urine is a serious business for the youngsters at a camp for diabetics. With the aid of a test kit, each child is able to determine the sugar level in his or her own urine.

The "raw" material of insulin is obtained from the pancreases of pigs and cows whose meat will be used for food. The pancreases are then processed in a pharmaceutical laboratory by complicated procedures of mashing, extracting the insulin, and removing impurities and the enzymes from the pancreatic tissue. Made suitable for injection as pure insulin in a liquid, it is then available sterile in rubber-stoppered bottles.

There are different kinds of insulin grouped according to how they act, how quickly they act, and for how long they work. Thus, there are Short (rapid acting), Intermediate (slow acting), and Prolonged (very slow) types. Insulin is supplied in three strengths—40, 80, and 100. The highest strength U–100—is now in wide use because the higher the concentration the smaller the quantity to be injected.

Andrea's prescription calls for an Intermediate type which begins working within 1 to 1½ hours. It acts for between 24 to 28 hours. The Intermediate types are used for persons getting one or possibly two injections a day. (They are not suitable in emergencies; instead, Regular insulin is used. Although Regular acts for a shorter time, it begins to work sooner and is appropriate for crises.)

Andrea gets 26 of U–100—20 in the morning, and 6 at six in the evening—of the Intermediate type. For her, as well as for any other person, the amount of insulin as well as the type of insulin is always determined by the doctor. With ex-

Insulin injections are a fact of daily life for most young diabetics.

perience, however, the diabetic can usually adjust the amount of insulin to take each day, consulting the doctor only when a problem arises.

WHAT'S FOR BREAKFAST?

We can surely say what breakfast will *not* be. It will not be a heaping bowl of sugar-coated cereal, two doughnuts, a banana, and hot chocolate. Andrea requires the same total calories in foods that provide the necessary proportions of protein, carbohydrates, fats, vitamins, and minerals that other children need for good health and normal growth. However, she breakfasts on what she knows will keep her diabetes in control. Her sugars and starches must balance her insulin for every meal. Other people don't worry about that because enough insulin will be produced automatically to take care of an occasional overloading of sweets and fats. Lots of sweets take the place of foods of better nutritional quality; besides, they are not good for the teeth.

Andrea's breakfast menu today might read something like this:

orange juice: ½ cup (125 ml)
dry (flaked or puffed cereal): ¾ cup (170 g)
bread or toast: 1 slice
whole milk: 1 cup (250 ml) to include on cereal

Tomorrow, the next day, and the rest of the mornings, her breakfast can be as varied as anyone else's. Her fruit choice could be: apple juice (⅓ cup [82 ml]); prune juice (¼ cup [62 ml]); half of a small banana; a peach; two tablespoons of raisins; or other possibilities. These selections and amounts are on a long list called *Exchange Lists for Meal Planning*. (More about that in another chapter.)

Her lunch in school or brought from home, as well as her dinner, are not likely to be different from the meals prepared for the rest of the family. Andrea does not require a special diet or "diabetic foods." And what is a good meal for her will also be nutritious, balanced, varied, and tasty for them too. Nor does it matter if the family is accustomed to Italian, Swedish, Chinese, Jewish, Mexican, American, or British. She can even indulge in an occasional pizza if that is a treat for the entire family.

A few good rules for the diabetic are: 1) eat when you feel hungry; if dinner is not ready, have a snack; 2) never skip a meal; 3) eat more when anticipating strenuous exercise; 4) stay away from concentrated sweets, for example chocolate bars, rich cakes and pastries, sweetened soft drinks, and seconds of desserts, unless it is fresh fruit.

"SNACKING" COULD BE A MUST

Snacks between meals are important to maintain a continuous supply of food to balance the injected insulin. In the non-diabetic, insulin production is turned off when no food is taken. There is no such "shut-off valve" in the diabetic. The choice of snacks is wide: cheese or peanut butter crackers, nuts, raisins, prunes, or dried apricots.

EXERCISE: ALSO IN BALANCE

Children do not have to be told to exercise. For Andrea, too, it is normal to play, run, skip rope, ride a bike, swim, skate and take part in physical education classes at school. Exercise stimulates the circulation, rushes glucose and oxygen to

[25

the brain, increases strength, promotes the growth of muscles and bones, and keeps one from getting flabby, overweight, and lazy.

For Andrea, it means one other thing. During exercise she burns up sugar and reduces her need for insulin. If she exercises too much, her blood sugar will fall. This will make her hungry and she will need a snack to restore her blood glucose. If she misses exercise, her blood sugar may go up and her amount of insulin will need to be increased. Exercise should therefore be regular and not exhausting.

The keystone of control is the *balance* of food, insulin, and activity.

Chapter 6
DIABETIC EMERGENCIES: TWO OPPOSITES

In diabetic shorthand, EDI stands for the daily balance of *E*xercise, *D*iet, *I*nsulin. If this threefold set of life necessities gets out of balance, control unwinds, and an emergency arises from either too low or too high blood sugar.

EMERGENCY 1:
IS IT HYPOGLYCEMIA?
AND WHY?

Have you gone too long without food? Have you skipped a meal? Was your breakfast too skimpy? Have you overreached your limit during recess activities? Was there no time for a snack? Or, could you have made a mistake and injected too much insulin?

Regardless of which of these things caused your blood

sugar to fall, you will know it by the way you feel. You have learned to recognize the danger signals: you are hungry, headachy, faint, perhaps a little nervous, trembling, and sweating. These are all uncomfortable reminders that you failed to strictly follow your prescribed daily schedule.

What to Do?

Reach for a quick sugar source: have a glass of orange juice, a piece of chocolate, or sweet soda pop. They will get glucose rushing to your blood and give you rapid relief from the frightening effects of running out of body fuel. It is absolutely necessary that diabetics always carry some quick source of sugar in their pocket or purse.

Insulin Reaction

When the first signs of hypoglycemia are not promptly reversed, the condition moves from discomfort to danger. Drowsiness and mental confusion set in and could lead to convulsions and unconsciousness, a full-blown insulin reaction! The unconscious person is unable to swallow. For immediate aid in this emergency, if it occurs at home or in school, administer Instant Glucose. Instant Glucose does not have to be swallowed. Someone should squirt it out of the tube, like toothpaste, and into the pouch of the cheek. It will be absorbed directly through the membrane lining the mouth. If glucagon is on hand, it should be injected by a trained individual into the skin to counteract the insulin and release glucose from the stored glycogen in the liver. It will work only if there is indeed a stored supply. If this does not restore consciousness within minutes, the person should be rushed to the doctor or to a hospital emergency room where glucose will be given in the vein.

EMERGENCY 2:
HYPERGLYCEMIA

If today your mouth is dry and you have an unquenchable thirst, if you are urinating more often than usual, feel weak, have stomach cramps, don't feel like eating, and are nauseated, you are heading for the opposite emergency—hyperglycemia. Did you neglect to take your insulin? Or, have you been a bit careless by either overeating at meals or at snacktime, so that you took in more than could be safely covered by the insulin injection? This reaction could also happen even if you have done everything to stay in control. If you are ill, have an injury, or are upset about something in school or in your family, your insulin requirement may be greater.

The symptoms of hyperglycemia may come on slowly, sometimes over a day or two, and do not strike with the suddenness of hypoglycemia. Vomiting, generalized pains, and difficulty in breathing may develop into a state of *coma.* In this state, one cannot be aroused by stimulation that would normally rouse one from a deep sleep. In a diabetic coma there is a state of *ketoacidosis.* Its literal meaning is *ketone* and *acid* wastes in the blood. Here is how it happens.

The body derives its energy mainly from carbohydrates and partially from fats. But if there is insufficient insulin, glucose burning is diminished, and the tissues call on the body fat reserves. Fats burn more slowly and incompletely, and the by-products of this incomplete oxidation are fragments of the fat modules—the ketones. They pile up in the blood, and are cast off by the kidneys. Most ketones are acids. They are excreted in the urine combined with alkali drawn from the blood, which reduces the normal alkalinity of blood. One of the ketone bodies spilling over into the urine is *acetone,* which escapes also through the lungs. The breath may then have a "fruity" sweet smell easily recognized as a sign of impending coma.

FIRE UP WITH GLUCOSE

The first step to combat ketosis is to give Regular insulin in moderate doses at short intervals to spark the burning of glucose in the cell furnaces. Just as in the spilling of sugar, the excretion of ketones in the urine also draws excessive water from the blood and then from the tissues. The tissues become even more dehydrated by the vomiting. The loss of water, salts, and alkali produces derangement of the body chemistry and requires heroic measures in a hospital. There, doctors will neutralize the acidosis by appropriate solutions introduced into the veins.

But all that is the doctor's business in a life-threatening emergency. Prevention is the job of the diabetic person. The diabetic has the lifetime job of staying in control, especially when sickness strikes, even if it is "only a cold."

SPECIAL RULES
ON SICK DAYS

On sick days, even though you are eating less, not exercising, resting in bed, and taking the usual number of insulin units, illness may throw your body out of balance. You may require more insulin. If the urine tests positive for sugar and also for ketone, a call to the doctor is a *must.* The doctor will determine how much extra insulin you need, and ask you to keep in close touch.

NEVER LEAVE HOME
WITHOUT YOUR ID TAG

Either of these two kinds of emergencies, hypoglycemia or hyperglycemia, may occur at any time or in any place. So your diabetic identification tag is your passport to prompt help. It will say: I AM A DIABETIC. My name is ————; my home telephone number is ————; my doctor's is ————. Or, get me to a hospital immediately.

Chapter 7
WHEN ADULTS
GET DIABETES

Mrs. Pickett, age 50, visited her doctor because of some vague symptoms. She felt weak; her body ached; she was bothered by itching in the vaginal area; and sometimes she felt a numbness or tingling in her fingers and toes. Time and again she had been advised to lose weight, but she failed to do so.

During the examination the doctor discovered sugar in her urine. Mrs. Pickett has been known to finish off a box of chocolates at one sitting; so she could have been having a temporary spill-over of sugar. But in view of her complaints, her obesity, and her age, the doctor ordered what is called a *glucose tolerance test.* She was asked to appear in the laboratory in the morning, *before breakfast.*

Her tests indicated that her body did not properly handle sugar. This confirmed the diagnosis of *maturity-onset,* or *diabetes mellitus.* In this type of diabetes, there is ineffective delivery, but not a total lack of insulin.

Mrs. Pickett is one among those four-fifths of all diabetics who are overweight. This does not mean that all obese persons are necessarily diabetic. Nor does it imply that a lean person is safe from developing the disease. It does indicate that obesity challenges the insulin utilization capacity, and often masks the diabetes which may go unnoticed until a much later age.

THE DOCTOR'S DECISION

The doctor has more leeway in prescribing treatment for the maturity-onset diabetic than for the child with juvenile diabetes. He starts Mrs. Pickett on a regimen designed for weight loss. He puts her on a diet. She must eat foods which are low in calories: no sweets, fewer starches, such as bread, spaghetti, noodles, potatoes, and rice. She also has to cut back on fats, such as butter, lard, salad oils, fatty meats, and fried food. As a guide, the doctor hands Mrs. Pickett a diet sheet that spells out what she may eat and what she must avoid. She will have to weigh herself every day, count her caloric intake, and take regular daily exercise. As she loses weight, she will be able to increase the amount of exercise, and in turn, she will find it easier to lose weight. She must return to the doctor's office in a month for more tests.

Suppose there is not enough improvement and the hyperglycemia persists, as is often the case in overweight diabetics. Her doctor may then decide on a second plan to control her diabetes. He would probably prescribe one of several drugs in the class of *oral hypoglycemic* agents. This would not be instead of but along with continued dietary control. Some of these drugs are chemicals related to the sulfa drugs, but they do not act against bacteria. Taken by mouth, these drugs lower the blood glucose by stimulating the release of insulin.

But this is effective only when the person still has some insulin-producing cells. That is why the drugs are not useful in juvenile diabetes. They do not substitute for insulin, nor do they act in the same way.

When the first of the oral hypoglycemic drugs was introduced in 1957, it was greeted by diabetic patients and their physicians as a happy deliverance from insulin injections. After a number of years, a government-funded study was reported to have shown that the later complications of diabetes (such as heart disease) occurred with greater frequency in patients on these pills than in those on diet and insulin.

The study, known as the University Group Diabetes Program (UGDP), was carried out in twelve American cities on 1,000 patients. As a result, the United States Food and Drug Administration has been attempting to require the drug companies to put a warning on the oral-drug label. This has outraged physicians who claim that their experience does not bear out the reported results and that interference with the use of the drugs would harm the well-being of about 1.5 million patients treated with this type of medication. Moreover, within recent months, when the details of the study were disclosed, diabetes specialists have asserted that the study was poorly conducted and its conclusions full of shocking flaws.

If the oral sugar-lowering drug does not control the diabetes, the last line of defense is insulin. The maturity-onset diabetic then also becomes insulin-dependent and has to follow the same rules as the young diabetic. He or she must take the regular injections in the amount and at the time prescribed; test the urine daily for sugar and ketone; strictly adhere to his or her diet; and exercise regularly. Any straying from the regimen may lead to a diabetic emergency.

SPECIAL EFFORT
NOT SPECIAL DIET

The maturity-onset diabetic, as well as the insulin-dependent person, does not need a "diabetic" or other "special diet." However, controlling the food intake by adults, particularly those with a tendency to become overweight, may require exercising greater discipline. They should restrain their appetite for high-calorie foods and eat more raw vegetables such as lettuce, celery, and cabbage.

Here are a few principles to guide you in menu planning.

1. Your diet should provide the total number of calories to maintain your desired body weight for your age, sex, height, occupation and physical activity. A woman working at a desk needs fewer calories than a "round-the-clock" homemaker of the same age, height, and body frame.

2. Most foods are mixtures of carbohydrate, fat, and protein. Foods high in fat should be taken sparingly. This is because a gram of fat furnishes nine calories, and a gram each of protein and carbohydrate yields four.

3. Stay away from fried foods. Instead, eat lean baked, boiled, broiled, or grilled meats.

4. As an aid to meal planning, become acquainted with Food Exchange Lists (prepared by the American Diabetes Association and the British Diabetes Association).

According to the Food Exchange System, foods are divided into six groups: 1) milk; 2a) vegetables (leafy green); 2b) vegetables (carrots, peas, beets); 3) fruits; 4) breads; 5) meat; 6) fats (butter, margarine, oils). The foods in each group are listed by the amount or size of portion.

YOUR DAILY DIET

Free foods and vegetables

Fruit exchange

Fats and oils exchange

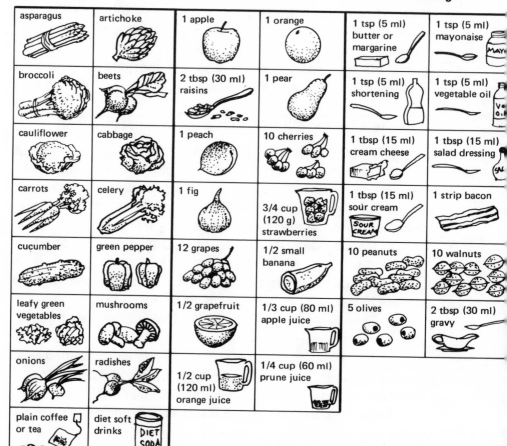

Free foods and vegetables		Fruit exchange		Fats and oils exchange	
asparagus	artichoke	1 apple	1 orange	1 tsp (5 ml) butter or margarine	1 tsp (5 ml) mayonaise
broccoli	beets	2 tbsp (30 ml) raisins	1 pear	1 tsp (5 ml) shortening	1 tsp (5 ml) vegetable oil
cauliflower	cabbage	1 peach	10 cherries	1 tbsp (15 ml) cream cheese	1 tbsp (15 ml) salad dressing
carrots	celery	1 fig	3/4 cup (120 g) strawberries	1 tbsp (15 ml) sour cream	1 strip bacon
cucumber	green pepper	12 grapes	1/2 small banana	10 peanuts	10 walnuts
leafy green vegetables	mushrooms	1/2 grapefruit	1/3 cup (80 ml) apple juice	5 olives	2 tbsp (30 ml) gravy
onions	radishes	1/2 cup (120 ml) orange juice	1/4 cup (60 ml) prune juice		
plain coffee or tea	diet soft drinks				
1/2 cup (120 ml) tomato juice					

Protein exchange

1 oz (28 g) beef	1 oz (28 g) liver	1 oz (28 g) turkey	1 oz (28 g) lamb chop
1 oz (28 g) pork chop	1 oz (28 g) hamburger	1 oz (28 g) chicken	1 slice cheese
1 egg	1/4 cup (40 g) tunafish	1/4 cup (40 g) salmon	1/4 cup (40 g) cottage cheese

Starch exchange

1 slice bread	1 biscuit or roll	1 pancake	1/2 cup (80 g) cooked cereal
3/4 cup (120 g) dry cereal	3 cup (720 g) popcorn	1 ear of corn	1 baked potato
1/2 cup (80 g) mashed potato	1/2 cup (80 g) noodles	1/2 cup (80 g) rice	1/2 cup (80 g) peas or beans

Milk exchange

1/2 pint (240 ml) whole milk	1/2 pint (240 ml) low fat milk
1/2 pint (240 ml) skim milk	8 oz (240 ml) plain yogurt

YOUR DAILY MEAL PLAN

LEGEND

One fruit exchange = 40 calories— 10 grams carbohydrate.

One starch exchange = 68 calories— 15 grams carbohydrate, 2 grams protein.

One milk exchange = 170 calories— 12 carbohydrate, 8 grams protein, 10 grams fat.

One protein exchange = 73 calories— 7 grams protein, 5 grams fat (1 meat exchange = 1 oz. meat).

One fat exchange = 45 calories— 5 grams fat.

Free food and vegetables may be eaten as desired.

	Breakfast	Snack	Lunch	Snack	Supper	Snack
Fruit						
Starch						
Milk						
Protein						
Fat						
Free Food & Vegetables						

A sample dinner menu based on the Exchange List could be:

hamburger, 3 exchanges, 3 ounces (85 g)
mashed potato, ½ cup (113 g)
spinach, as much as desired
carrots, ½ cup (113 g)
bread, 1 slice
butter; 1 level teaspoon
apple, large
coffee or tea

Or Exchange List Equivalent

roast beef (lean), 3 ounces (85 g)
peas, ½ cup (113 g)
broccoli, as much as desired
bread, 2 exchanges; omitting mashed potato
butter, 1 level teaspoon
peaches (water packed)
coffee or tea

Through practice, when the diabetic is sufficiently acquainted with the equivalent food values and portions, he or she need not consult the list for every meal or even every day. It is possible to choose from a wide variety of foods on these long lists and maintain a diet reasonably uniform in quantity and quality.

One can be confident that the diet for the diabetic will be equally nutritious for the other members of the family. As well, it can readily be adjusted to suit individual taste and ethnic preferences.

Chapter 8
COMPLICATIONS
OF A COMPLICATED
DISEASE

Diabetes is not a simple disease. Even when kept under control for years it eventually takes a heavy toll in some individuals. As the diabetic grows older, chronic complications set in. These problems involve nearly all the organs and systems.

PROBLEMS OF CIRCULATION

After a time, diabetes produces changes in the blood vessels. In non-diabetics these changes are usually associated with growing old. It has been said that maturity-onset diabetics age more quickly than non-diabetics. The large arteries lose their normal elasticity, the walls stiffen, and the vessels become narrower in diameter. The inner layer, normally smooth, thickens and becomes irregular with *plaques,* deposits of fatty and other materials. This deterioration, known as *atherosclerosis,* comes on earlier in a person with diabetes. As a result, the blood flow is reduced and slowed. This impairs the

[39

functions especially of the heart, the brain, the kidneys, and the legs.

Also the capillaries, the tiny vessels which deliver the blood to the tissues, become diseased. Their walls weaken, the blood flow slackens, the vessels leak or become plugged, and sometimes burst, causing hemorrhages. A hemorrhage in the brain causes a stroke, in the heart a heart attack, and in the eyes impaired vision and in some cases blindness. Because of poor circulation, cuts, sores and wounds heal slowly and become infected more easily.

THE NERVES IN DIABETES

Damage to the *peripheral* (outlying) nerves cause abnormalities of nerve function in various ways in different parts of the body. It is as if damage to the fat-like layer leaves the inner conducting part exposed. This causes a "short-circuiting" of the nerve impulses, somewhat like worn insulation on an electric cord produces a short circuit.

Feelings of numbness, burning, crawling, or stabbing pains in the feet and toes are often symptoms. The soles may be sensitive to touch, pressure, or vibration, which makes walking uncomfortable. On the other hand, a person may *lose* his or her sense of pain and temperature sensation. In this case, the person is subject to injury from bumping, stepping on a thumbtack or nail, or coming in contact with a hot object.

DEVASTATING EFFECTS ON THE EYE

Different parts of the eye are vulnerable. Hyperglycemia increases the glucose concentration in the lens and in the *vitreous,* the clear, jelly-like substance inside the eyeball.

[40

This causes a dimming of vision, and the sensation of seeing through smoke. More serious are the circulatory complications, such as hemorrhages. The blood vessels may become twisted and widened in spots and then bulge out into balloons and obstruct vision. Breaks in the vessels on the surface of the retina eventually form small scars. If the burst vessels are replaced by new vessels bunched around the *macula* in the middle of the retina, then blindness results. For diabetics under poor control, these complications may begin to develop some fifteen or more years after the onset of the disease. For diabetics under better control, these problems may arise after three or four decades.

Diabetologists stress that these ravages can be reduced and postponed in patients who have maintained good control and have avoided episodes of ketoacidosis. Diabetic retinopathy is more likely to be a complication if the diabetic has neglected his or her care and has experienced recurrent infections and other stressful conditions which have caused blood sugar imbalances.

THE KIDNEY AND SKIN

Two conditions—poor circulation and a predisposition to infection—leave their mark on the kidneys of diabetics. Structural changes impair the filtering function of the kidneys, and this could ultimately lead to kidney failure.

Skin infections are extremely frequent if the diabetic is in poor control. Common staph infections occur much more often than in non-diabetics, and unless they are promptly treated with antibiotics, the process may result in ulcers.

It cannot be stressed too often that strict control of glucose in the blood, prevention of infection, and prompt attention to cuts, sores, and bruises are imperative for the

[41

health of the diabetic. Today it is often pointed out that a person with diabetes, more constantly watchful of his care, is likely to be in better health than a non-diabetic. Jack Benny, a diabetic, died at 80. He did not die from diabetes, but cancer. He said in a TV interview at age 72 that he attributed his health and energy to good control of diabetes through proper diet, regular exercise, and good living.

FOOT CARE

Proper care of the feet is important for diabetics of all ages. Tight or otherwise ill-fitting shoes may cause problems, such as corns. One reason why these become major foot problems in the diabetic is because the blood supply to the feet is cut down especially in this area. Another reason is that nerve damage may occur. The feet should be inspected every day for danger signs: redness, swellings, cracks in the skin, sores, and the buildup of hard, rough skin. These should be treated by a doctor specializing in foot care, and you should not cut or trim them back with a razor blade or knife. The doctor should be told you are a diabetic. He or she will then be your physician for foot care.

Your doctor will be sure to give you a list of Do's and Don'ts, such as: file toenails straight across; bathe feet daily in lukewarm (not hot) water with mild soap; dry your feet gently, especially between toes. Your socks should be heavy, cotton, free of seams and darns and, of course, the correct size. Your shoes should be soft leather, and new ones must be "broken in" slowly. Going barefoot is not for the diabetic, especially if the feet would be exposed to rain, cold, or excessive sunlight. Walking, with comfortable shoes, leather soles, and flat heels, is the exercise for the adult diabetic.

Chapter 9
LIVING A LIFETIME WITH DIABETES

Brian's parents felt shattered when they learned that he had diabetes. The doctor's assurance that with appropriate care he could lead a full and active life did not soften the jolt. How were they going to cope with the management of this terrifying illness in a two-year-old? The very thought of having to inject insulin into him daily gave his mother cold shivers. And just how much food will balance the insulin? And suppose he throws up, what then? How will she know whether he is having an insulin reaction or he is just having a tantrum? Getting a urine specimen from a baby not yet fully toilet trained would in itself be quite a trick, she thought.

CHILD AND FAMILY ADJUSTING TO DIABETES

For Brian's parents, the early years of adjusting to the demanding daily care of their diabetic child were trying. Finding the urine positive for sugar on some days—quite usual in children—was unnerving. Such anxieties were not lost on Brian. When his mother was shaky he had reason to cry and did. And that did not help his diabetes. For his parents, it was difficult to be calm even at such minor "crises," but with time the family settled in and accepted the routines.

Then, during Brian's growing years, the family faced other emotional problems. His mother was worried that Brian might eat all the chocolate in his Easter basket. Sometimes his brother and sisters were irked when he had to be fed while they had to wait for dinner to be ready. For Brian it was no fun to have shots twice a day. And he couldn't understand why he had to refuse the lollipop the barber offered him after his haircut. He would play on his parents' concerns, and they would be over-protective. But coddling would not give him the self-confidence to make friends. Brian had to learn not to dominate his home. He and the rest of the family would have to accept his diabetes. He needed to develop independence and to be prepared for the time when he could assume some responsibility for his own care. Then his diabetes would not prevent him from sleeping over at a friend's house, going on an overnight trip with his scout troop, or taking trips planned for the family. Going to a summer camp for diabetic children when he was eight made him more accepting of his diabetes; also, being away from the constant watchful eye of his concerned mother gave him greater self-confidence.

HOW DIFFERENT ARE YOU?

For diabetic teenagers, adolescence brings problems over and above those faced by non-diabetics. At times they may feel set apart from their peers. They tend to nurse gripes and feel sorry for themselves: They might think, "How normal is my life anyway? I cannot forget my insulin. I must pack my syringe and urine-testing paraphernalia on excursions away from home. I must worry about not 'cheating' on that diet. And do I tell the kids about my diabetes when my blood sugar is high and I have to make many trips to the toilet?"

Other gnawing questions arise. "Can I be honest with my date, when I say I have to eat on time, and will the truth end it all? Is smoking out for me? Must I turn down a beer at that party? Will I be able to be licensed to drive a car?"

If a wholesome relationship has been built up with the parents, honest and reassuring answers will be forthcoming. But there are times when an adolescent will feel freer in a talk with the doctor than with anyone else. The doctor is likely to be more convincing when he or she reiterates that diabetes is not a defect. The physician will probably say, "Accept it and you will find you can do lots of things you thought you could not do." The doctor might even cite a true story reported in *Diabetes Forecast* about a young woman who became diabetic at 17 and at 25 biked 100 miles (161 km) in one day in "The Century Ride." Mary Tyler Moore, baseball's Ron Santo, tennis pro Billy Talbert, and hockey star Bobby Clarke are living proof that diabetics can live active and exciting lives.

WHAT ABOUT A CAREER?

"What choices do I have?" Count the ones closed to diabetics. Insulin-dependent persons are excluded from military service. They are not permitted to pilot aircraft or drive public vehicles in interstate commerce. Police work, fire-fighting, and jobs calling for work on scaffolds or involving high-speed ma-

[45

chinery are not for diabetics. But look at the choices wide open: medicine; research in all the sciences; art; music; theatre; engineering; advertising; photography; journalism; education; computer technology; religion; civil service work, to name just a few.

Cathy plans to become a doctor. She excels in her science courses, and has time for extracurricular activities. She coaches gymnastics, and plays the clarinet in the high school band. Cathy's older brother Wayne has had diabetes since he was eight. As a child he made aircraft models and carved wooden animals. Later, he did drift-wood sculptures, for which he won prizes. Now he earns his living refinishing fine antique furniture, and his hobby is sleight-of-hand magic.

ADULTS WITH DIABETES
HAVE CONCERNS TOO

When the diabetic marries, the marriage partner should fully understand what diabetes is, what problems may arise, and how to cope with problems and emergencies. Should diabetics consider having a family? If the decision is not to have children, is the Pill the right method of birth control for the diabetic woman? The doctor is likely to warn that birth control pills are hormones which tend to raise the blood sugar. That means that the woman's insulin needs would have to be watched even more closely. A diabetic woman must understand that pregnancy puts greater than usual physical and emotional stress on her, which makes it more difficult to control the diabetes. Is pregnancy a risk to the diabetic woman? Will the child be healthy? She must be prepared for very special prenatal care to avoid the risks that existed forty or more years ago.

Will the diabetic man or woman be able to get life insurance? The adult with diabetes under good medical control can today obtain a life insurance policy, but at a higher cost. The insurance company considers the age of the applicant, the duration of the diabetes, and the presence or absence of complications in setting the amount of the insurance and the premiums that will be charged. An insurable diabetic may be confident of providing economic security for the family. Also, he or she can live a long and productive life. History records that, despite his diabetes, statesman Georges Clemenceau, among others, made a contribution in a demanding career and reached the age of 88. Writer H. G. Wells lived until 80.

At the age of 35, Dr. George R. Minot suddenly developed all the symptoms that would have alarmed him in one of his patients. With the half-measures available in 1920, he lived on a starvation diet, weighed every morsel of food, and measured every mouthful. Dr. Minot was working against time when insulin was discovered. Then he was able to dispense with the little table scales. He went on with his work and found a remedy for another life-threatening disease—pernicious anemia. For his discovery he won the Nobel Prize. He lived to be 65.

The concerns of diabetics are often troublesome. For example, through ignorance, some employers are still prejudiced against diabetics. But the more the diabetic learns about his or her diabetes, the better he or she can control it. Thus, the diabetic is able to demonstrate to non-diabetics that a diabetic can perform as well as anyone else equally qualified in his or her field.

Chapter 10
RESEARCH
DIRECTIONS TODAY

Diabetic research is wide in scope and directed to explore all aspects of the disease. Broadly, it is aimed to improve treatment, stop the devastating complications, find the cause (or causes), discover a cure, and help implement means of prevention. Prevention will probably be achieved only through basic research. It even may occur in areas which seem remotely related to diabetes. For example, the latest and most dramatic discovery—how to produce human insulin —grew out of sophisticated research in genetics.

In the mid 1960s, basic research based on immunologic principles led to the development of a method sensitive to measuring the quantities of hormones, among them insulin. The normal fasting level of insulin is measured in micro-units (a micro-unit is one millionth of a unit). This method made it possible to measure the degree of insulin deficiency in a person. Also, it contributed significantly both to progress in insulin research and to a means of distinguishing between moderate diabetics and non-diabetics. For this work, Dr. Rosalyn Yalow was one of the recipients of the 1977 Nobel Prize in Medicine and Physiology.

The two others who shared that prize—Drs. Roger Guillemin and Andrew Schally—in a totally different investigation, discovered a hormone produced in a part of the brain known as the hypothalamus. This hormone inhibits the secretion of the growth hormone. They called it *somatostatin* from the Greek *soma,* meaning "body," and *statin,* "to stop," to describe its inhibiting action. Found in many tissues, including the pancreatic islets, somatostatin inhibits glucagon, which causes the blood sugar to fall. The possibility exists that somatostatin might be useful in the treatment of diabetes.

A BOOST TO BASIC RESEARCH

In 1973, a group of concerned parents of children with diabetes met in Philadelphia and chartered the Juvenile Diabetes Foundation. They were convinced that the way to a cure early in the disease—before its ravages take their toll—must come from research. And if a cure came before discovery of cause, basic research would be the road to success. Determined in their effort to open the trail, they lobbied the United States Congress to increase government spending in this area. At the same time, the Foundation itself undertook to raise funds. Today the funding by JDF and by the older American Diabetes Association supplements the amount allocated by Congress for diabetes research. The boards of these voluntary agencies consist of medical experts and lay people. They select and sponsor scientists to work on research proj-

[49

ects. As a result, research in diabetes has received enormous impetus toward new projects. As well, projects begun before the formation of JDF have been given a boost.

PROJECTS
IN THE WORKS

One aim is to find a way to relieve the diabetic from the pain and drudgery of life-long injections of insulin. A device which may some day permit automatic insulin delivery to control the blood sugar level is the *artificial pancreas*. Based in part on technology developed for space exploration and in part on medical technology, such as the cardiac pacemaker, this plan involves an implantable packet.

Placed under the skin, the packet would contain a tiny sensor to sample the blood for glucose level, a miniature pump, and a computer to signal the pump to deliver insulin into the blood as needed. While work on an implantable pancreas is continuing, a portable pancreas has become available for trial.

The *portable pancreas* is a device attached to a belt and is designed to be worn by the child with diabetes. It consists of a miniature battery-driven pump that normalizes the blood sugar in those diabetics who have difficulty in maintaining control without wide swings in either glucose or insulin levels. It injects insulin under the skin round the clock on a preset individual schedule, and injects extra doses before meals and snacks. The portable insulin pump is still in the experimental phase while experts watch how it works in a handful of children wearing it during their normal day at home, school, and play.

 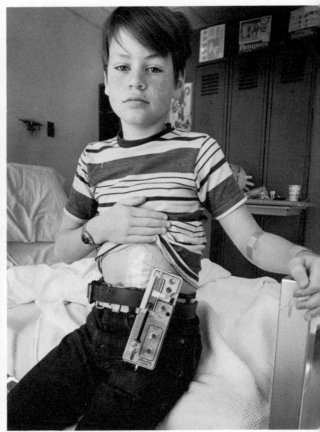

Scientists hope that an artificial pancreas like the one pictured here (left) will one day eliminate the need for insulin injections. This portable pancreas (right) provides insulin at a steady rate during both day and night. Though still in its experimental stages, it has proven helpful in keeping the sugar level normal in some patients.

PANCREAS TRANSPLANT?

Could a whole pancreas be transplanted, like a heart or kidney? Efforts to transplant a pancreas have not met with much success. There is the problem, as with other grafts, of the body rejecting it. In addition, a way would have to be found to dispose of the pancreatic juice which destroys insulin.

More promising is the possibility of transplanting clumps of cells from the pancreas of a fetus lost before the pregnancy was completed. Experiments in rats show that the transplanted beta cells do control the blood sugar. When grown first in culture, they are less subject to rejection. If the technical problems can be solved, this could be a major breakthrough.

HUMAN INSULIN VIA GENETIC ENGINEERING

The method by which human insulin was produced involved a process called *recombinant DNA,* a kind of gene splicing following the transference of genetic material from one species to another to alter the gene of the latter. DNA (the abbreviation for *deoxyribonucleic acid*) contained in the chromosome of each cell carries the hereditary blueprint, or genetic instructions, for making the vast number of body proteins including insulin. The genes, which determine what we are, what we look like, and how we behave, are strung on the long spiral, coiled, two-stranded DNA molecule. One gene directs the synthesis of a single protein.

A team of scientists from two laboratories in California transferred the gene from the DNA of islet cells into the DNA of a bacterium, *Escherichia coli.* This bacterium, which inhabits the intestine, was especially bred to live only in the laboratory. By using a special enzyme and a very complicated procedure, the genes of bacterial DNA were snipped out. A fragment of DNA for the gene for human insulin, similarly "dissected out" and restructured was slipped into the gap in the bacterium DNA. The bacterium with the altered gene makes copies of itself in a nutrient culture. It then could be grown in vats to manufacture insulin—*human insulin!* Recent reports indicate that this human insulin will soon be produced in quantities large enough to sell. It will help those diabetics who are allergic to animal insulin. Besides, with diabetes on the rise, there is some danger that insulin from animals will be in short supply. Putting bacteria to work to mass-produce insulin could solve both problems in the near future.

CLUES IN THE SEARCH OF A CAUSE

Researchers have found a specific antibody in the blood of children with diabetes. It latches on to the surface of the islet cells and inactivates them much in the way that antibodies to different disease-causing viruses destroy the foreign invader into the body. It is as if the immune system in diabetes becomes disordered and mistakenly attacks the body's own cells. Could something like this be a cause of diabetes? If so, what triggers the immune system to go wrong?

Other work done in the United States and in Great Britain has shown that a number of viruses—the mumps virus and Coxsackie B, for example—destroy the islet cells. Perhaps other viruses which cause common childhood diseases similarly destroy the beta cells.

[53

A WEAPON TO ARREST
A COMPLICATION

When diabetic retinopathy occurs, the damage cannot be reversed. Nevertheless, it can be checked to prevent ultimate blindness. By a process introduced about two decades ago, an intense beam of light is focused into the eye to destroy weakened blood vessels to prevent hemorrhaging. The process, known as photocoagulation, seals off those blood vessels. While it does not restore vision in that part of the retina, it prevents more damage to the area of central vision and prevents blindness from serious bleeding. More recently, the laser beam has replaced photocoagulation because it can be very accurately focused on the spot to be treated.

Thanks to the financial support of talented researchers by various organizations, and to government grants, we may look forward with optimism to continued advances in the field of *diabetes mellitus.*

Glossary

ACETONE: A product of faulty fat oxidation that appears in the urine of a diabetic.

ALPHA CELLS: Cells in the islets of the pancreas that produce a hormone—glucagon—which works in the opposite way from insulin to convert glycogen to glucose.

AMINO ACIDS: The building blocks of proteins.

ARTIFICIAL PANCREAS: A device containing a miniature pump designed to inject insulin under the skin round the clock, to maintain normal sugar levels in diabetics. It is often attached to the patient's belt.

ATHEROSCLEROSIS: Abnormal condition in which the lining of the arteries thickens. It occurs earlier in diabetics, and is one of the complications of the disease.

BETA CELLS: Cells in the islets of the pancreas that produce insulin.

CARBOHYDRATES: One of the three organic foodstuffs; common name for starches and sugars.

COMA: The result of severe deficiency of insulin; a state of unconsciousness from which the diabetic cannot be aroused by stimulation.

DIABETES MELLITUS: The name of the disease in which sugar appears in the urine due to deficiency of insulin.

FOOD EXCHANGE SYSTEM: Lists of foods showing equivalent foods that the diabetic can substitute to satisfy normal dietary needs.

GLUCAGON: The hormone produced in the islets of the pancreas that converts liver glycogen to glucose.

GLUCOSE: The name for a simple sugar.

GLUCOSE TOLERANCE: The degree to which a person can handle glucose without a spill-over in the urine.

GLYCOGEN: A complex carbohydrate, sometimes called "animal starch"; the form in which the body stores carbohydrates.

HORMONE: A substance produced in endocrine glands, distributed by the blood to some organ in the body, the function of which it regulates.

HYPERGLYCEMIA: A condition of high blood sugar.

HYPOGLYCEMIA: A condition in which the blood sugar in the blood is below normal.

INSULIN: The hormone produced by the beta cells in the islets of the pancreas needed for utilization of sugar by the body.

INSULIN-DEPENDENT: A person whose diabetes can be controlled *only* by insulin.

INSULIN REACTION: A symptom of excess insulin in the blood—faintness, trembling, and sweating, which may lead to convulsions and shock if not treated promptly by taking sugar in some form.

INSULIN UNIT: The quantity of insulin crystals contained in one unit of liquid, regardless of the type of insulin prescribed.

[56

ISLETS OF LANGERHANS: Clumps of special cells in the pancreas that produce insulin.

JUVENILE DIABETES: Present in both children and adults who are insulin-dependent.

KETOACIDOSIS: A condition of the blood due to accumulation of ketones, acid waste from incompletely burned fats.

MATURITY-ONSET DIABETES: That type of diabetes occurring in persons who become diabetic in middle age or later. They are usually not insulin-dependent.

ORAL HYPOGLYCEMIC DRUGS: Drugs taken by mouth which lower the blood sugar. Cannot be given to insulin-dependent diabetics.

PLAQUES: Deposits of fat and other accumulations in the lining of the large arteries—a condition in atherosclerosis.

POLYDIPSIA: Excessive thirst, one of the three major symptoms in untreated diabetes.

POLYURIA: The excretion of enormous amounts of urine— another major symptom in diabetes.

PROTEINS: Nitrogen-containing organic foodstuffs required for building and repairing all tissues. Absolutely necessary for growth.

RECOMBINANT DNA: A process of gene splicing. It has been used to transfer the gene from DNA of islet cells into DNA of bacteria to produce human insulin. (DNA, contained in the chromosome of each cell, carries the hereditary blueprint for making all body proteins.)

SOMATOSTATIN: A recently isolated hormone produced in a part of the brain; it inhibits secretion of the growth hormone. It is thought that by inhibiting the production of glucagon, it could lower the blood sugar, and therefore possibly be useful in treating diabetes.

[57

Further Reading

BOOKS

Bierman, June and Tohey, Barbara. *The Diabetes Sports and Exercise Book, How to Play Your Way to Better Health.* Philadelphia: J. B. Lippincott, 1977.

Boylen, Brian Richard and Weller, Charles, M.D. *The New Way to Live With Diabetes.* New York: Doubleday, 1976.

Court, John Maurice. *Helping Your Diabetic Child.* New York: Taplinger Publishing Co., 1975.

Fajans, Stefan S., ed. *Diabetes Mellitus.* Washington, D.C.: Department of Health, Education and Welfare (HEW), 1976.

Goodman, Joseph I., M.D. with Biggers, W. Watts. *Diabetes Without Fear.* New York: Arbor House, 1978.

Jorgensen, Caryl D. and Lewis, John E. *The ABC's of Diabetes.* New York: Crown, 1978.

[58

Krall, Leo P., ed. *Joslin Diabetes Manual.* 11th ed. Philadelphia: Lea & Febiger, 1978.

Loewenstein, Bertrand E. and Preger, Paul D., Jr. *Diabetes, New Look at an Old Problem.* New York: Harper and Row, 1976.

MAGAZINES

Diabetes Forecast
A publication of the
American Diabetes Association, Inc.
600 Fifth Avenue
New York, NY 10020

PAMPHLETS

Booklets on diabetes can be
obtained by writing to:

American Diabetes Association
600 Fifth Ave.
New York, NY 10020

Juvenile Diabetes Foundation
23 East 26th Street
New York, NY 10010

The Joslin Diabetes Foundation
c/o The Joslin Clinic
One Joslin Place
Boston, MA 02215

Index

Acetone, 29–30, 55
Adolescence, 44–45
Adults, 6, 8–9, 17, 32–36, 46–47.
   See also Aging
Aging, 39–40
Alpha cells, 13, 55
American Diabetes Association, 49
Amino acids, 10, 13, 55
Antibodies, 53
Aretaeus, 2
Artificial pancreas, 50, 51, 55
Asians, 6
Atherosclerosis, 39–40, 55

Bacterium, and DNA, 52–53
Banting, Frederick, 12
Benny, Jack, 42
Best, Charles, 12
Beta cells, 13, 52, 55
Birth control, 46

Black African, 6
Blindness, 41, 54
Blood, 2, 3, 12, 13, 14, 26, 33–34.
   See also Circulation; Hypergly-
   cemia; Hypoglycemia; Insulin
Books, 58–59
Brain, 17
Breakfast, 24

Carbohydrates, 4, 5, 8, 55
Careers, 45–46
Children, 1–3, 5, 6–9, 17, 50; and
   lifetime care, 18–26; living with,
   43–46
Circulation, 39–40, 41, 42
Clarke, Bobby, 45
Clemenceau, Georges, 47
Collip, James, 12
Coma, 29, 30, 55–56
Complications, 39–42

Coxsackie B virus, 53

Diabetes Forecast, 45
Diabetes mellitus, defined, 56
Diet. *See* Food
DNA, 52–53, 57
Dogs, 11, 12
Drugs, 33–34, 57

Egyptians, 2
Elderly, the, 6. *See also* Adults
Emergencies, 27–31
Escherichia coli, 52–53
Eskimos, 6
Exercise, 18, 25–26, 34, 42
Eyes and blindness, 40–41, 54

Family, 7–8, 43–44, *See also* Heredity
Fatigue, 17
Fats, 5, 16, 29, 33, 35
Food (diet), 2, 4–5, 11, 12–13, 24–25, 33, 34, 35–36. *See also* Hunger
Food and Drug Administration, 34
Food Exchange Lists, 35–36, 56
Foot care, 42

Genes and genetics, 6, 52–53
Glucagon 13, 28, 49, 56
Glucose, 4–5, 13, 14–16, 17, 56. *See also* Blood; Hyperglycemia; Hypoglycemia; Urine
Glucose tolerance, 32, 56
Glycogen, 5, 13, 28, 56
Glycosuria, 16
Greek physician, ancient, 2
Guillemin, Roger, 49

Heart disease, 34
Hemorrhages, 40, 41, 54
Heredity, 5, 6
Hormones, defined, 56
Hunger, 11, 16–17
Hyperglycemia, 14, 29–30, 31, 33, 40–51, 56. *See also* Blood
Hypoglycemia, 27–28, 31, 56
Hypothalamus, 49

ID tags, 31
Indians, Asian, 6
Infections, 41–42. *See also* Viruses
Instant Glucose, 28
Insulin, 2, 5, 6, 8, 10–13, 18, 21–23, 26, 33–34, 56; and emergencies, 28, 30; and research, 48–49, 50, 52–53
Insulin-dependent, defined, 56
Insulin reaction, defined, 56
Insulin unit, defined, 56
Insurance, 47
Islets of Langerhans, 11, 12–13, 49, 52–53, 57

Japanese, 6
Juvenile Diabetes Foundation, 49
Juvenile-onset diabetes, 8, 9, 17, 57. *See also* Children

Ketones, 16, 19, 29–30, 34. *See also* Ketosis
Ketosis (ketoacidosis), 29–30, 57
Kidneys, 14, 29, 41

Laser beams, 54
Life insurance, 47

Magazines, 59
Maturity-onset diabetes, 8, 9, 39–40, 57. *See also* Adults
Metabolic disorder, diabetes as, 5
Minot, George R., 47
Moore, Mary Tyler, 45
Mumps, 53

Nerves, 40
Nobel Prize, 12, 47, 49

Oral hypoglycemic drugs, 33–34, 57
Orientals, 6
Overweight (obesity), 6, 8, 32, 33

Pancreas, 5, 8, 10–13, 22, 49; artificial, 50, 51, 55; transplant, 52
Photocoagulation, 54
Plaques, 39, 57
Polydipsia, 16, 57
Polyuria, 16, 57
Portable pancreas, 50, 51
Pregnancy, 46
Proteins, 5, 10, 57

Recombinant DNA, 52–53, 57
Research, 46–54
Retinopathy. *See* Eyes and blindness

Santo, Ron, 42
Schally, Andrew, 49
Shoes, 42
Sick days, 30
Skin, 41–42
Snacks, 25
Somatostatin, 49, 57
Sugar, 1–2, 3. *See also* Blood; Glucose; Urine

Talbert, Billy, 45
Thirst, 1, 2, 10, 16, 29
Tissue hunger, 16–17

University Group Diabetes Program, 34
Urine (urination), 1, 2, 4, 11, 14–15, 18, 19–20, 29, 30, 32, 34
Viruses (viral infections), 5, 53

Walking, 42
Weight, loss, 17. *See also* Overweight
Wells, H. G., 17

Yalow, Rosalyn, 49